Enchanting Earth Science

Lakshmi Narayani

About the Book

Enchanting Earth Science includes the following topics:

- Four Seasons
- Solar System
- Moon Phases
- Water Cycle
- Rock Cycle
- Landforms

This book starts with a lyrical narrative about each of the Earth Science topics. This is followed by a fact sheet section with interesting facts about the topic and a section for fun activities for children related to the topic.

The activities include creating a mind map, answering quiz questions, solving a word puzzle and coloring. Fact sheet represents the important terms/concepts in a tabular format, the mind map explains the concept pictorially and word games, quiz and coloring reinforce the learning.

Creation of Mind maps as a learning aid will come in very handy for the kids and this book has sample mind maps created. Mind map creation can be applied to any learning topic.

This is a very handy tool for the teachers to teach about the Earth Science topics and also a good tool for homeschooling.

Author Biography

Lakshmi Narayani is an IT professional. She holds a Masters degree in commerce and has worked in the IT industry for 13 years. She grew up in India and currently lives in Atlanta. She used to be the neighborhood nanny before she started her career and enjoyed spending time with children. She is a mother of a preschooler girl and enjoys teaching and learning with her daughter.

When she is not managing IT projects, she spends time with her daughter and husband, writes and works on the web site that she is creating for children. Her technical articles have been published in magazines and seminars but writing educational books for children in a simple and fun manner has been her vision which has resulted in the series of educational books on various topics that are presented in a fun to read, easy to remember format.

To Mahima and Srikanth

Contents

1. Learn about the Four Seasons

The Four Seasons Song

Four seasons a year in range

Come one after the other

Seasons come then seasons change

This happens every year

Changes in Seasons

Happen for good reasons

Knowing what happens

Shall be one of our good lessons

Earth spins around the sun

All thru the year

Sometimes far from the sun

And sometimes very near

The axis of its rotation and tilt

And the angle of sunshine

Cause the changes in the weather

And the days to be shorter or longer

Names of the seasons

Let's know them all

Winter, Spring, Summer and Fall

Winter, Spring, Summer and Fall

It's Winter...It's Winter

It's cold and snowy Winter

It's time to get the Warm clothes out

Wear your coats, mittens and boots before you venture out

Many trees shed their leaves and covered with snow or icicles

And it's Christmas time – oh merry time, lets sing Jingle Bells

Time for skiing or sledging or just making your own Snow Man

And when the new year is here, you can have as much fun as you can

It's Spring...It's Spring

It's Warm and stormy spring

Coats and Mittens can be packed up nice and dandy

But keep a couple of layers and your sweatshirts handy

Sow your seeds and plant your saplings - it's time for gardening

Leaves sprout and flowers bloom – that's the beauty of Spring

And its Easter time – oh what fun time, to look for eggs from Bunny

Run outside and enjoy the weather which is now warm and sunny

It's Summer...It's Summer

It's hot and sunny Summer

Get your tank tops, shorts, swimsuits and sunglasses out

Put on sunscreen before you step out and for thunderstorms you better watch out

Swimming, Cycling, Camping and Running are some cool things to do

Head to the Park or Beach or holiday spot – where there is so much to do

Schools are closed – so make the most of this time

But do not forget to finish your holiday home work on time ☺

13

It's Fall…It's Fall

It's cool and windy Fall

Get those scarves and boots and umbrellas out

Time to add a few layers before your step out

Leaves change colors – yellow, orange, red and different shades thereof

Trees shed leaves everywhere – so rake those leaves that fall off

Get back to school and start the lessons for the next grade

And enjoy dressing up and join the Halloween parade

Names of the seasons

Now we know them all

Winter, Spring, Summer and Fall

Winter, Spring, Summer and Fall

Four Seasons: The Fact Sheet

A **season** is a division of the year marked by changes in weather, ecology and hours of day light. Seasons result from the yearly revolution of the Earth around the Sun.

The earth's axis is tilted about **23.5** degrees, so the Earth is never straight up or down compared to the Sun. Due to this, during winter the sun's highest point in the sky is very low.

The seasons are caused as the Earth, tilted on its axis, travels in a loop around the Sun each year.

Summer happens in the hemisphere tilted towards the Sun, and winter happens in the hemisphere tilted away from the Sun.

As the Earth travels around the Sun, the hemisphere that is tilted towards or away from the Sun changes. The hemisphere that is tilted towards the Sun is warmer because sunlight travels more directly to the Earth's surface so less gets scattered in the atmosphere. That means that when it is summer in the Northern Hemisphere, it is winter in the Southern Hemisphere.

 The hemisphere that is tilted towards the Sun has longer days and shorter nights. That's why days are longer during the summer than during the winter.

The Four Seasons Table

Season	Temperature	Weather/ Environment	Dressing Style	Activities
Spring	Warm	Rainy, Stormy Flowers Bloom, Leaves Sprout	Less Layered Dressing, Sweat Shirts	Sow Seeds, Gardening
Summer	Hot	Sunny, Heat Waves, Thunderstorms	Shorts, Tank Tops	Swimming, Camping, Cycling, Fun in the Park/beach, Holiday trips
Fall / Autumn	Cool	Rainy, Windy, Leaves changing Colors, Leaves fall	Layered dressing, Scarves, Boots	Raking Leaves
Winter	Cold	Snowy, Frost, no Leaves	Many layered dressing, Scarves, Hats, Coats, Mittens, Snow Boots	Skiing, Sledging

Activity 1: The Four Seasons Mind Map

Refer to the below pictorial map explaining the four seasons and create your own map that will help you remember them always!

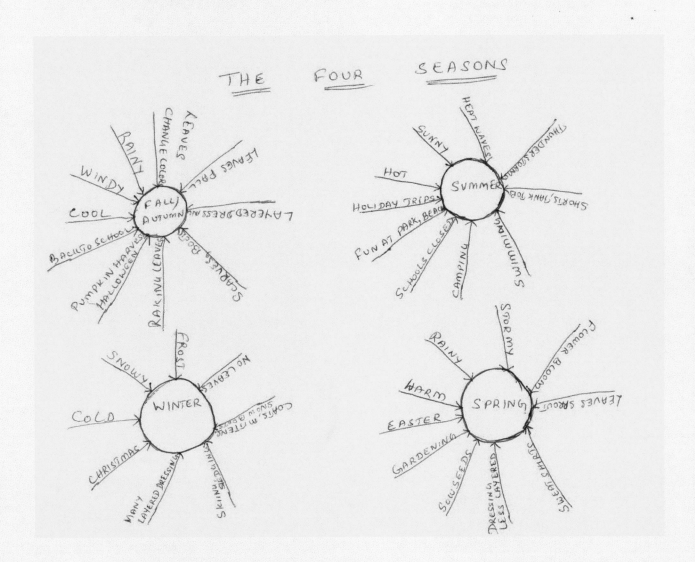

Activity 2: The Four Seasons Quiz

1. Which season is cold and snowy?

Answer:

2. Which season is Hot and Sunny?

Answer:

3. Which season is Warm and Stormy?

Answer:

4. Which season is Cool and Windy?

Answer:

5. Name the season during which the leaves change colors.

Answer:

6. Which season requires many layered dressing?

Answer:

7. Which season would have you wearing sunglasses, shorts and tank tops?

Answer:

8. Which season is good for sowing seeds and Gardening?

Answer:

9. Which season is good for skiing and sledging?

Answer:

Activity 3: The Four Seasons Word Game

p	g	S	j	t	c	i	S	a	s	S	e
s	f	u	F	a	l	l	u	j	n	n	s
a	g	n	i	r	p	S	m	t	e	o	l
m	g	n	b	a	r	p	m	k	e	w	f
t	d	y	m	l	a	z	e	f	w	y	c
s	i	j	x	x	y	n	r	m	o	z	w
i	e	z	m	k	d	m	p	q	l	d	b
r	m	q	j	v	l	z	z	u	l	q	b
h	n	p	g	d	c	o	t	q	a	x	c
C	s	n	o	s	a	e	S	b	H	z	e
k	a	l	l	g	u	i	i	r	j	f	a
u	r	e	t	n	i	W	W	i	n	d	y

1. Seasons

2. Winter

3. Summer

4. Spring

5. Fall

6. Halloween

7. Christmas

8. Windy

9. Snowy

10. Sunny

Activity 4: Color and name the Four Seasons

Color the picture with the characteristics of your favorite season.

2. Learn about the Solar System

The Solar Anthem

Sun's family is called the solar system

This song about them is called the solar anthem

Sun is the biggest and brightest Star

Spinning around it are the planets near and far

Eight planets spin around the sun

Learning about them is so much fun

Mercury, Venus, Earth and Mars are the Inner Planets

Jupiter, Saturn, Uranus, Neptune are the Outer Planets

Asteroids, Comets, Meteoroids, Plutoids are the small objects

They all go around the sun in circular and elliptic orbits

Mercury is the closest and the heavy weight

It has no atmosphere and no moons in sight

Venus is hot and dry with many volcanoes

It has no moons that anyone ever knows

Earth is the densest and our dearest

It has one Moon, many Oceans, Trees and people that never rest

Mars is the Red Planet; it is dry and cold

It has 2 moons and that's what we are told

Jupiter is the biggest and a stormy Planet

It has 50 moons and a few more that do not count yet

Saturn is the least dense and the light-weight

It has 62 moons and a ring that stands out in the light

Uranus is cold and has a tilted axis

It has 27 moons but there are no taxis

Neptune is cold and windy

It has 13 moons that are nice and dandy

Pluto is a Dwarf Planet that does not count anymore

It has 3 moons and will be known as a Plutoid in the future folklore

Ceres, Eris, Haumea and Makemake are the other small planets

Adding Pluto to this list makes a total of Five Dwarf Planets

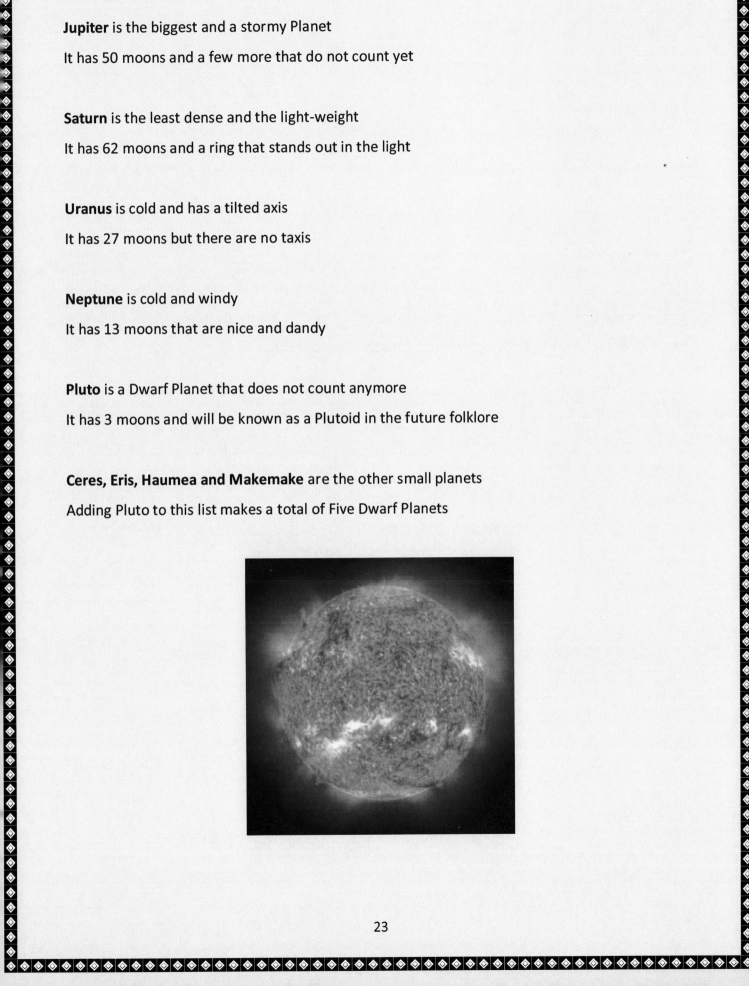

Solar System: The Fact Sheet

What is Astronomy?

Astronomy is a natural science that studies celestial objects such as planets, comets and galaxies.

The Solar System

The Solar System is made up of the planets, moons, comets, asteroids, meteoroids, dust and gas. Everything in the Solar System orbits or revolves around the Sun.

The Sun

Name	Key Facts
Sun	• The Brightest and biggest star • Eight Planets and other small objects revolve around the sun in space

Inner Planets

Planets	Colors	Orbit	Moons	Key Facts
Mercury	Orange	Elliptical	None	No atmosphere, Heavy planet
Venus	Yellow	Circular	None	Many Volcanoes, Dry, Hottest Planet
Earth	Blue, Brown, Green	Circular	1	Has Rocks, Oceans, trees, Animals, People, Densest Planet, Moon is called Luna
Mars	Red	Circular	2	Dry and cold, Red Planet

Outer Planets

Planets	Colors	Orbit	Moons	Key Facts
Jupiter	Yellow, Red, Brown	Circular	50+	Stormy, Biggest Planet
Saturn	Yellow	Circular	62	Light-weight, Least dense, second largest planet with rings
Uranus	Blue, Green	Circular	27	Cold, Has tilted rotation axis
Neptune	Blue	Circular	13	Cold and Windy planet

Plutoids

Name	Orbit	Moons	Key Facts
Pluto	Elliptical	3	Coldest, Dwarf Planet
Ceres	Circular	0	Dwarf Planet
Eris	Elliptical	1	Moon is named Dysnomia
MakeMake	Elliptical	0	Dwarf Planet
Haumea	Elliptical	2	Dwarf Planet

Small objects

Small Objects	Key Facts
Asteroids	Minor Planets, Rocky, Asteroid belt is between Mars and Jupiter
Comets	Small, icy bodies with very long tails
Meteoroids	Small/tiny bodies travel through space, stony / metallic, smaller than asteroids

Activity 1: The Solar System Mind Map

See the sample mind map below about the solar system. Create your own map to remember key facts about solar system.

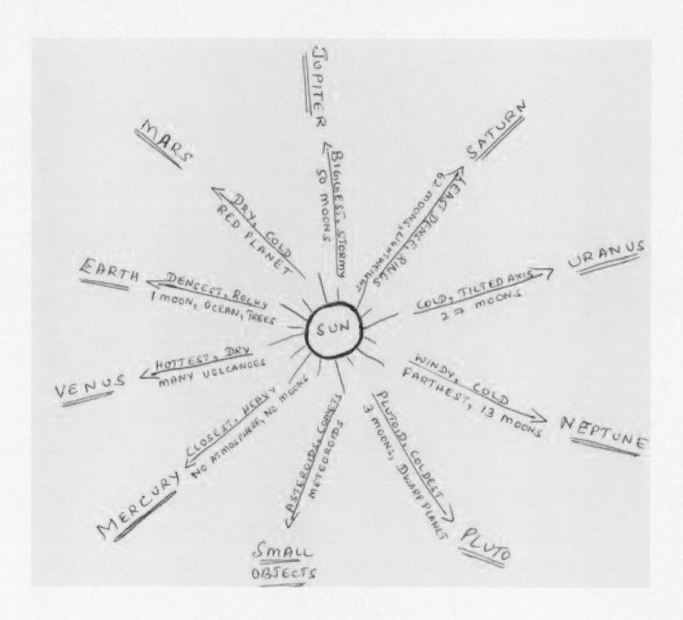

Activity 2: The Solar System Quiz

1. How many Planets are in the solar system?

Answer:

2. Which is the biggest star in the Solar System?

Answer:

3. Which is the Stormy Planet in the Solar System?

Answer:

4. Which Planet has rings?

Answer:

5. Which is the biggest planet in the solar system?

Answer:

6. Which is the hottest planet in the solar system?

Answer:

7. Which Planet is closest to the Sun?

Answer:

8. Which planet is farthest from the Sun?

Answer:

9. What was once called a Planet but not anymore?

Answer:

10. Which Planet has Oceans, Rocks, Trees, Animals and People?

Answer:

11. Name the Inner Planets in the solar system

Answer:

12. Name the Outer Planets in the solar system

Answer:

13. Name the small objects in the solar system

Answer:

14. Name the Planet with the tilted axis?

Answer:

15. Name the Windy Planet?

Answer:

Activity 3: The Solar System Word Game

S	N	M	E	T	C	O	P	A	N	T	M	H	A	F
O	M	I	N	N	E	R	P	L	A	N	E	T	S	S
S	L	S	E	O	P	L	I	L	O	H	E	R	G	U
U	A	T	N	Y	M	O	N	O	R	T	S	A	E	N
N	T	E	P	I	I	A	R	E	A	S	B	E	X	A
E	S	N	S	A	L	B	T	R	P	D	G	O	G	R
V	D	A	C	L	I	I	A	P	L	L	K	J	C	U
H	I	L	T	T	P	O	P	L	U	T	O	I	D	S
N	O	P	M	U	J	N	E	P	T	U	N	E	L	S
R	R	R	J	D	R	U	L	C	O	M	E	T	S	A
A	E	E	A	S	B	N	R	L	H	V	E	N	A	S
E	T	T	S	T	L	A	C	I	T	P	I	L	L	E
D	S	U	M	E	T	E	O	R	O	I	D	S	C	V
O	A	O	Y	S	I	A	T	P	L	O	S	E	S	N
L	A	M	E	T	S	Y	S	R	A	L	O	S	O	U

Find the below words hidden in the word square above.

1. COMETS
2. PLUTO
3. STAR
4. SOLARSYSTEM
5. ORBIT
6. ASTEROIDS
7. INNER PLANETS
8. OUTER PLANETS

9. NEPTUNE
10. ELLIPTICAL
11. ASTRONOMY
12. MERCURY
13. VENUS
14. EARTH
15. MARS
16. JUPITER

17. METEOROIDS
18. URANUS
19. PLUTOIDS
20. SATURN

Activity 4: The Picture Game - Name the planets and objects

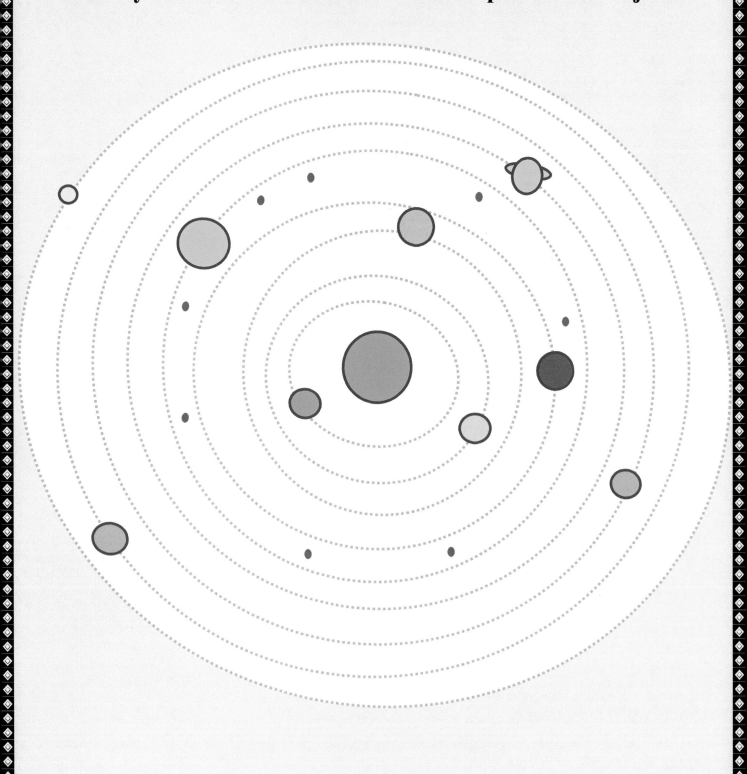

3. Where did the Moon go...?

The Moon Song

Child

Oh dear Moon, where did you go from the sky?

I see the Sun but not you and I wonder why?

Are you running away from the Sun?

Or are you swimming under the Ocean?

Moon

Oh dear Child - I am still up in the sky, alright

Orbiting the Earth – be it day or night

You can't see me during the day very well due to the bright sunlight

Check back after the sun sets and you'll see me shining through the night

Child

Oh dear Moon, where did you go from the sky?

The Sun is gone but you are still not seen and I wonder why?

Are you hiding behind the clouds?

Or are you visiting another planet and making rounds?

Moon

Oh dear Child - I am still up in the sky, alright

Orbiting the Earth – be it day or night

When I go around the Earth and come in line with the Sun

You can't see me from where you are but I am not on the run

Child

Oh dear Moon, where did you go from the sky?

The Sun is gone - I see but only a Crescent and I wonder why?

Are you wearing a cloak?

Or are you playing hide and seek?

Moon

Oh dear Child - I am still up in the sky, alright

Orbiting the Earth – be it day or night

When I go around the Earth and move ahead of the Sun's direct line

You see me reflecting the Sun's light as I peek showing the little crescent of mine

Child

Oh dear Moon, how come you have many names?

The Sun has one but you seem to have many sizes and shapes

Are you a sorcerer that can grow and shrink at will?

Or are you running in and out of the moon saw mill?

Moon

Oh dear Child - I have but one Sphere shape but I do have many a form and name

New moon when I vanish, Full moon when full, Crescent and Gibbous when I wax and wane

When I go around the Earth, in and away from the line of the Sun

I seem to grow, shrink and disappear as I reflect more or less of the light from the Sun

Oh dear Child - I am still up in the sky, alright

Orbiting the Earth – be it day or night

Oh dear Child - I am still up in the sky, alright

And that is where I always am – be it day or night

Moon Phases: The Fact Sheet

The Moon is the only natural satellite of the Earth and the fifth largest satellite in the Solar System.

- Moon constantly orbits around the Earth. It takes 27.3 days to complete one elliptical round. However, since the Earth is moving in its orbit about the Sun at the same time, it takes slightly longer for the Moon to show the same phase to Earth, which is about 29.5 days.

- It orbits the Earth counterclockwise – West to East

- Moon rises in the East and sets in the West

- Moon has many craters, mountains and valleys but no atmosphere

- Moon does not make any light on its own. It just reflects the sunlight

- Sunlight always illuminates one side of the Moon

- Though it appears from the Earth that the shape of the moon is changing everyday is driven by how much of the light reflection can be seen based on where the Moon's position is in its Orbit around the Earth and where it is located from Sun's direct line

- As the moon rotates around the earth, it also rotates around its own axis at the same rate. This is why we always see the same side of the moon.

- **Blue Moon** as in "Once in a Blue Moon…" does not refer to the color of the moon but it refers to the second full moon occurring within a calendar month. This occurs once every three years on an average.

- The changing shape of the bright part of the Moon that we see is called its phase.

- There are various Moon phases depending on how it is seen from the Earth

  - When the bright part is a full circle, it is Full Moon

  - When the bright part if not seen at all, it is New Moon

  - When the bright part is getting bigger, the Moon is Waxing.

  - When it is getting smaller, the Moon is Waning.

  - When the Moon is more than half-lit, it is called a Gibbous Moon.

  - When the moon is less than half-lit, it is called a Crescent Moon.

- The New moon occurs when the moon and the sun are on the same side of Earth. The moon is between the Sun and the Earth and therefore the moon does not reflect the sunlight.

- The Full Moon is when the Earth is between the sun and the moon and the brighter side of the moon reflecting the sunlight stays visible from the Earth throughout the night.

How to identify the Moon Phase?

To identify whether the Moon is waxing or waning is easy. Step outside when the sun is about to set and look at the sky. If you do not see the moon then, check again later at night.

If the Moon is already seen in the sky before Sun set, then the Moon is waxing. Every night it will rise a little later in the day and look a little fuller. At Full Moon it will rise almost exactly when the Sun sets.

If the Moon is not seen in the sky at night fall, but long after sunset, then the Moon is waning. Every day it will rise a little later and look a little thinner. At New Moon it will rise almost exactly when the Sun rises, but you won't be able to see it at all.

The Moon Phases Table

Moon Phase Name	Description
Full Moon	The Moon's side that is completely illuminated by the sunlight is facing the Earth. The Moon is seen from the Earth clearly shining brightly in the sky.
Waning Gibbous	The Moon appears to be more than one-half but not fully illuminated by direct sunlight. The fraction of the Moon's disk that is illuminated is slowly decreasing day by day.
Last Quarter	One-half of the Moon appears to be illuminated by direct sunlight. The fraction of the Moon's disk that is illuminated is slowly decreasing day by day.
Waning Crescent	The Moon appears to be partly but less than one-half illuminated by direct sunlight. The fraction of the Moon's disk that is illuminated is slowly decreasing day by day.
New Moon or Dark Moon	The Moon is in direct line with the Sun and the side of the moon that is not illuminated by the Sunlight is facing the Earth. The Moon is not visible (except during a solar eclipse).
Waxing Crescent	The Moon appears to be partly but less than one-half illuminated by direct sunlight. The fraction of the Moon's disk that is illuminated is slowly increasing day by day.
First Quarter	One-half of the Moon appears to be illuminated by direct sunlight. The fraction of the Moon's disk that is illuminated is slowly increasing day by day.
Waxing Gibbous	The Moon appears to be more than one-half but not fully illuminated by direct sunlight. The fraction of the Moon's disk that is illuminated is slowly increasing day by day.

Activity 1: The Moon Phases Mind Map

Refer to the below pictorial map capturing different phases of the Moon and create your own map that will help you remember them always!

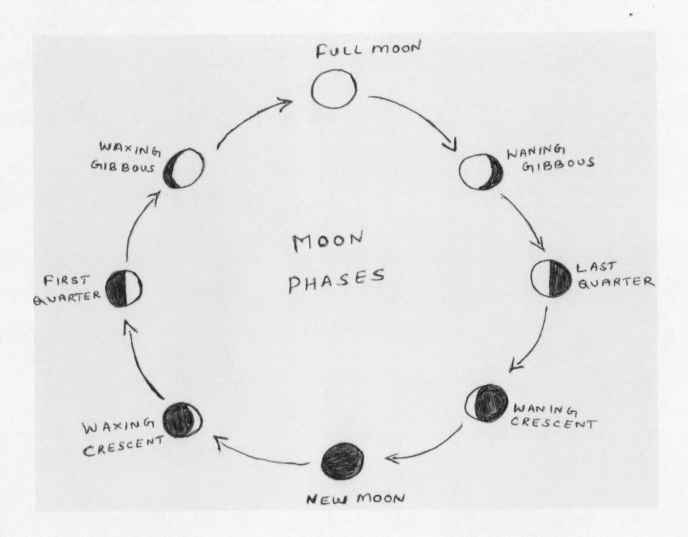

Activity 2: The Moon Phases Quiz

1. Why is the moon mostly not visible during day time?

Answer:

2. How many days does the moon take to orbit around the Earth?

Answer:

3. What is a Blue Moon?

Answer:

4. Moon is the only natural satellite of the Earth – True or False?

Answer:

5. Moon rises in the west and sets in the east – True or False?

Answer:

6. When the moon seems to grow each day, the moon phase is known as ……

Answer:

7. When the moon seems to shrink each day, the moon phase is known as ……

Answer:

8. The Full Moon is seen when the Earth is between the sun and the moon – True or False?

Answer:

9. Why do we always see only the same side of the Moon from Earth?

Answer:

10. Does the moon actually grow and shrink in size?

Answer:

Activity 3: The Moon Phases Word Game

N	N	L	A	O	Z	K	J	V	N	C	B	N	C	B
n	e	g	n	i	x	a	W	R	E	K	V	A	H	J
o	w	T	T	U	G	H	I	Y	F	G	H	F	N	W
o	M	P	R	Z	G	O	Z	X	Q	E	U	M	H	B
M	o	H	A	S	D	H	J	G	M	n	U	J	D	t
e	o	C	F	R	E	E	S	C	Y	o	M	J	O	i
u	n	J	K	O	E	X	G	V	Z	o	C	r	X	b
l	e	t	i	l	l	e	t	a	S	M	r	e	O	r
B	M	G	J	I	B	T	Z	B	D	l	e	t	g	O
S	D	S	R	A	Q	S	B	L	H	I	s	r	n	P
K	V	Y	J	E	Y	A	J	H	H	u	c	a	i	K
D	S	T	R	B	P	G	C	S	H	F	e	u	n	P
R	s	u	o	b	b	i	G	N	F	G	n	Q	a	F
E	X	E	D	C	J	A	D	S	A	O	t	D	W	L
D	D	F	J	X	B	M	A	F	Z	B	E	D	O	I

1. Full Moon

2. New Moon

3. Crescent

4. Gibbous

5. Waxing

6. Satellite

7. Orbit

8. Waning

9. Quarter

10. Blue Moon

Activity 4: Color the Night Sky

Have fun coloring the night sky.

4. Learn about Water Cycle

The Story of a Water Drop

I am a little water drop

I live in the ocean Dippity Dop

I swim around under the shining sun

Sharing my story is so much fun

I play with my other Ocean friends

We rush as waves to find where the Ocean ends

We rise up high and hit the shore

And laugh out loud with a huge uproar

We swim and swim and swim and swim

And swim and swim and swim and swim

All the way around the Ocean

Until I got scorched under the hot sun

The sun's heat was too much to bear

Oh like magic, I became water vapor

Evaporation is the name of this process

And I traveled up to the sky under some stress

I went up and up and up and up

And up and up and up and up

All the way up to the sky

Until I felt the cold air hit me high

Cold air turns water vapor back to water

Oh like magic, I became a cloud shaped like an Otter

Condensation is the name of this process

And I float around in my new white dress

I float and float and float and float

And float and float and float and float

All the way around the sky

Until I saw my other Ocean friends passing by

We joined our hands and began to dance

This made the clouds turn so dark, if you take a glance

We kicked up a storm and clapped up a thunder

Now what will happen, you must wonder

I started falling down in the form of rain

Oh like magic, I became a water droplet again

Precipitation is the name of this process

And I raced down with my friends making a big fuss

I went down and down and down and down

And down and down and down and down

All the way down to the Earth

Until I mingled into a waterfall

I danced down to the stream

I passed thru all the places on my dream

In this last phase of the **Water Cycle**

And joined a river with a loud chuckle

I went zig and zag and zig and zag

And zig and zag and zig and zag

All the way through to the Ocean

Until I settled into my good old mansion

I lazed around and moved in vain

Oh like magic, I am home again

Collection is the name of this process

It's time for me to take a short recess

I live forever in different forms and shapes

As I cruise thru the ocean, sky and landscapes

Many consider me to be more precious than gold

My friends and I are seen all over the world

I swim, float, pour, runoff and flow

Sometimes fast and sometimes slow

In each form I take I have many uses

I quench thirst, water plants and I also clean your noses ☺

I love this journey - going up and down

And just can't wait to do it again!

This process is called the **Hydrologic cycle**

And this is my fun story going in circle!

Oh wait….my story does not end here

There are a few more things I have to share

When my journey goes on smoothly, I am happy

But when people make my homes dirty, I become sad and snappy

There are times when I cannot go back up

Due to many things that humans goof up

Deforestation, Farming, Pollution and Erosion

When these are done in excess they affect my motion

When I don't go up, I can't pour down again

This causes Drought which means no rain

Less water on surface impacts all life alike

And makes everyone suffer which I greatly dislike

You can make a difference, You can contribute

Use me wisely, Harvest rainwater and STOP pollution in my tribute

Help me go on my journey without a break hereafter

So that we all can live happily ever after!!

I am a little water drop

I live in the ocean Dippity Dop

I swim around under the shining sun

Sharing my story is so much fun

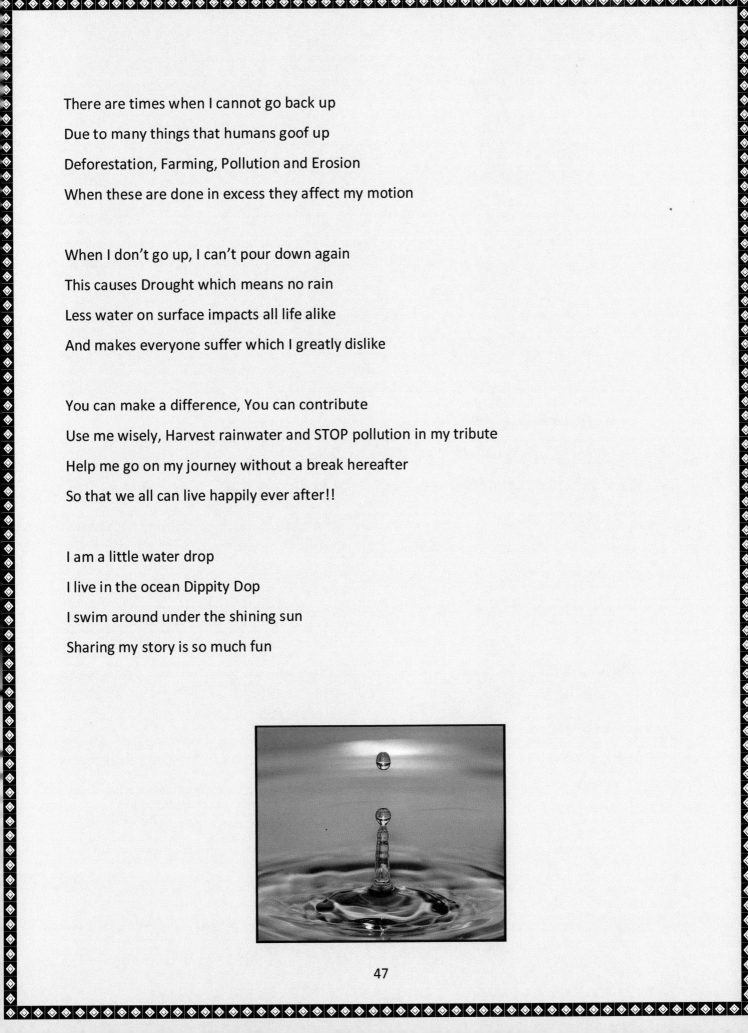

Water Cycle: The Fact Sheet

What is Water Cycle?

The process where water takes different forms during its journey from the land to the sky and back to land. It's called a cycle because it happens over and over again. This is also called Hydrologic cycle.

Water Facts

- About 70% of Earth is covered with Oceans. It amounts to roughly 326,000,000,000,000,000,000 gallons (**326 million trillion gallons**)
- 97% of all the water on Earth is in the Oceans. Only 2% is fresh water.
- Water is the most important substance on Earth. It fuels life. 65% of human body is made up of water
- It is vastly used for cleaning, cooking, irrigation, generating electricity, transportation
- All the water on Earth is constantly circulating - it evaporates from the ocean, travels up in the air, comes back to the land in the form of rain and flows back to the ocean.

Factors affecting Water Cycle

Factors affecting Water Cycle	Description
Over Farming	Over-farming is taking too much away from the land and not returning enough back. It can include depleting the soil of nutrients, lowering the water table, loss of soil through erosion (water or wind).

Factors affecting Water Cycle	Description
Deforestation	**Deforestation** is the removal of a forest / trees and converting that land for some other use – like building factories/shopping malls
Pollution	Water pollution is the contamination of water bodies like ocean, river, lakes with harmful compounds/chemicals

The Water Cycle Processes Table

Process	Form of Water	Cause of Transformation	Other Information
Collection	Liquid/ Water droplets	None	Water is collected in Oceans, Lakes, Rivers
Evaporation	Vapor	Heat from the Sun	Water from various collections evaporate and vapor travels up in the air
Transpiration	Vapor	Heat from the Sun	Water on the trees evaporate and travel up in the air
Condensation	Liquid/ Tiny droplets/Clouds	Cold air	Water vapor condenses back to liquid form in cold air and becomes clouds
Precipitation	Liquid / Water Droplets	High condensation in the air	Water in the clouds precipitate and fall down when there is high condensation and clouds become heavy

What you can do to help water life cycle?

Things to do to help Water Cycle	Description
Conserve Water	Using water wisely and reducing the amount consumed
Harvest Rainwater	Collecting and storing rain water from relatively clean surfaces such as a roof, land surface for later use instead of letting it go down the drain. The water is generally stored in a rainwater tank or directed into the ground to recharge groundwater
Stop Pollution	Not littering the water bodies, using pesticides and insecticides wisely

Activity 1: The Water Cycle Mind Map

Refer to the below pictorial map explaining the water cycle processes and create your own map that will help you understand the processes better and remember them always!

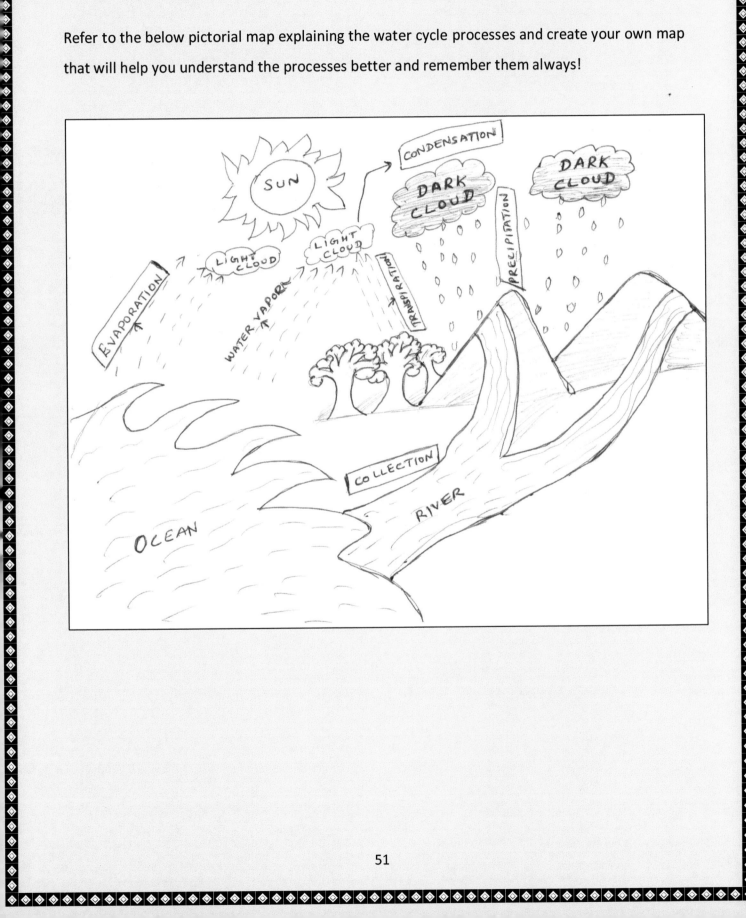

Activity 2: The Water Cycle Quiz

1. Water from the Ocean disappears and goes up in the air. What is this process?

    Answer:

2. Vapor is hit by the cold air and becomes tiny water droplets again. What is this process?

    Answer:

3. High condensation causes the clouds to rain. What is this process called?

    Answer:

4. Rivers, lakes, Oceans hold water on the land. What is this process called?

    Answer:

5. Trees release their water into the air due to Sun's heat. What is this process called?

    Answer:

6. What is the other name for Water Cycle?

    Answer:

7. What are the causes for Drought?

    Answer:

8. How much Water is available on Earth?

    Answer:

Activity 3: The Water Cycle Word Game

B	Y	K	P	U	Z	P	F	T	I	N	A	O	H	H	K	M
W	O	S	R	S	U	Z	P	A	K	D	V	H	O	X	E	n
W	l	e	v	r	e	s	n	o	C	J	Z	N	P	X	C	o
M	M	J	F	D	L	Z	V	V	A	Q	G	I	L	H	I	i
X	n	o	i	t	u	l	l	o	P	G	R	W	Z	T	T	t
D	e	f	o	r	e	s	t	a	t	i	o	n	X	K	O	a
n	K	P	F	H	Q	S	F	R	A	A	K	S	S	I	C	s
o	Q	U	P	K	B	U	A	R	K	E	Y	C	W	G	Z	n
i	e	l	c	y	C	c	i	g	o	l	o	r	d	y	H	e
t	E	v	a	p	o	r	a	t	i	o	n	X	F	e	X	d
c	G	E	T	H	Z	K	Y	B	C	W	E	K	M	n	S	n
e	J	T	D	K	G	Q	C	I	B	P	T	C	V	r	A	o
I	B	W	Y	L	W	Z	G	U	Y	M	I	B	J	u	E	C
I	Q	M	S	L	W	J	A	D	V	E	F	T	V	o	l	D
o	X	Q	R	M	U	E	A	H	N	W	V	K	A	J	D	O
C	n	O	i	t	a	t	i	p	i	c	e	r	P	U	R	B
D	r	O	u	g	h	t	M	C	I	F	C	T	Y	Q	I	V

Find the below words hidden in the above word square

1. Evaporation
2. Condensation
3. Precipitation
4. Collection
5. Hydrologic Cycle
6. Drought
7. Pollution
8. Conserve
9. Deforestation
10. Journey

Activity 4: Color and name the water cycle processes

Enjoy coloring the water cycle process.

5. Learn about the Rock Cycle

The Rock Cycle Song

Rock cycle goes beyond time in history

This song will help you unravel that mystery

Three types of rocks are Igneous, Sedimentary and Metamorphic

Rocks on Earth are ages old and their story is terrific

Earth is a rocky Planet with many depths and elevations

Digging deep into the Earth will give many revelations

Top layer of Earth is called the **Crust** and next layer is **Mantle**

Core is the deepest layer that is extremely hot for you to handle

Earth's Crust has many plates that move towards and apart from each other

This causes the continents to drift far away or stay together

Movement of these plates is called **plate tectonics**

It's a wonderful showcase of nature's histrionics

Super continents form and break apart over millions of years

Because the heat currents in Mantle cause the Crust to have many tears

Plate tectonics and Continental drifts make rocks to move up and down the earth

Rock cycle is the process causing rocks to be born and take many forms in each rebirth

Molten rock deep inside the Earth is called **Magma**

When the Crust tears, magma flows up and volcanoes put up a drama

Magma cools as it moves up and forms into **igneous rocks** that are exclusive

Igneous rocks on the crust are omnipresent and hey, that is conclusive

When magma cools below the surface, the igneous rocks are called **intrusive**

When lava cools on the surface, the igneous rocks are called **extrusive**

Mountains and Molehills erode in storms, rains and sunshine

Weathering is the name of the process that causes rocks to break and whine

Rock particles get deposited into river or ocean sediment beds by wind and water movements

And there igneous rocks, fossils, minerals cement together into **Sedimentary rock** monuments

As Igneous and Sedimentary rocks get pushed deeper into the Earth's hotter layers and cracks

The heat and pressure change their attributes as they morph into **metamorphic rocks**

Rocks that pass through the very hot layers of Earth melt and become Magma once again

Thus the rock cycle continues as Magma pushes up and new rocks are formed in the bargain

Three types of rocks are Igneous, Sedimentary and Metamorphic

Rocks on Earth are ages old, isn't their story terrific?

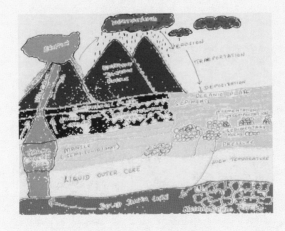

Rock Cycle: The Fact Sheet

What is Rock Cycle?

Rock Cycle is the process that forms and recycles different types of rocks on the Earth. To summarize this cycle – rocks begin as Igneous rocks, erode and cement into Sedimentary rocks, morph into Metamorphic rocks, melt into magma, cool down and solidify into Igneous rocks again.

Earth Facts

- Earth is made of Rocks and Minerals
- Earth is made up of many layers – Crust, Mantle, Outer Core and Inner Core
- Earth's core is extremely hot, around 7,200 degrees Celsius - which is hotter than the surface of the sun
- Movements in Continental and Oceanic plate push magma up and the rocks up/down
- 95% of Earth's crust is made of Igneous rocks
- Place where Magma erupts to the surface of the Earth is called a Volcano
- The crust is about 0.5 % of the earth's total mass.
- The crust is made up of silicate rocks such as granite and basalt.
- The Crust is made of 12 Continental and Oceanic plates that are very slowly and constantly moving towards and apart from each other due to the convection currents in the Mantle. Movement of these plate is called as Plate Tectonics
- Oceanic crust is made up of rock rich in iron and magnesium. These are primarily basalt formed by volcanic action at the mid ocean ridges. The oceanic crust is denser than continental crust.

- Continental crust is made up of igneous, metamorphic, and sedimentary rocks. The continental crust is less dense than the oceanic crust. When the continental crust collides with oceanic crust through plate movement the continental crust rides over the top of the oceanic crust while the oceanic crust is pushed back down towards the mantle.

- Formation of super continents and their breaking up over years is considered to be a cyclical phenomenon.

- Millions of years ago, the current continents were all part of a super continent called Pangaea that went through many phases of break up over the years until the time the continents are in their current locations

Rock Facts

- All rocks are made of minerals

- Three main categories of rocks are Igneous, Sedimentary and Metamorphic

- Igneous rocks are formed when Magma/Lava cools down and solidifies.

- When Magma cools down below the surface of the earth, Intrusive Igneous rocks are formed

- When Lava cools down on the surface of the earth, Extrusive Igneous rocks are formed

- Process of any liquid cooling into solid form is called Crystallization

- Type of Volcano also determines the type of rock formation

- Rock cycle spans over a very long period – it takes thousands and millions of years for the rocks to change forms

The Rock Cycle Table

Process	Rock Category	Rock Form	Cause of Transformation	Other Information
Melting	Any	Liquid	Heat in the Earth's Mantle / Core	
Crystallization	Intrusive Igneous Rock	Solid	Cooler temperature in Earth's crust	As Earth's crust pushes apart, Magma moves up from the Core/Mantle and the cooler temperature solidifies the molten rock
Eruption	Extrusive Igneous Rock	Solid	Cooler Temperature on Earth's surface	As Lava flows out from the Volcanoes, the cooler temperature on Earth's surface solidifies the molten rock
Weathering and Erosion	Igneous Rock	Solid	Water and wind cause the rocks to weather over time and erode	
Transportation	Igneous Rock	Solid	Wind and Water move the rocks from various places into sediment beds	Rocks break down into Sand/Soil, Clay, Silt, Mud, Dirt and Dust
Deposition	Igneous Rock	Solid	Rock particles are deposited into sediment beds	

Process	Rock Category	Rock Form	Cause of Transformation	Other Information
Cementing and Compacting	Sedimentary Rock	Solid	Different types of rock particles, fossils get cemented together and compacted due to pressure and chemical reactions of the minerals they are made up of.	
Metamorphism	Metamorphic Rock	Solid	High temperature and pressure cause the igneous and sedimentary rocks to change their properties	Igneous and sedimentary rocks that are transformed from their original attributes are known as metamorphic rocks
Melting	Any	Liquid	Heat in the Earth's Mantle/Core	And the cycle continues...

Rock Categories

Rock Category	Meaning of Rock category	Types of Rocks	Other Information
Igneous	Resulting from Fire and Heat	Granite, Basalt, Rhyolite	Intrusive Igneous rocks are formed when the magma cools down below the Earth's surface Extrusive Igneous rocks are formed when lava cools on the surface of the Earth
Sedimentary	Cementation of different types of rocks	Conglomerate, Breccia, Limestone, Gypsum, Shale, Sandstone	Conglomerate is made up of rounded rocks Breccia is made up of angled rocks Sedimentary rocks will contain fossils as they get cemented
Metamorphic	Form changing from original composition	Slate, Schist, Gneiss, Marble, Quartzite	Shale is transformed into Slate Limestone is transformed into Marble

Minerals found in different layers of Earth

Earth's Layer	Minerals Found
Crust	Oxygen, Magnesium, Aluminum, Silicon, Calcium, Sodium, Potassium, Iron
Mantle	Silicon, Oxygen, Aluminum, Iron
Core	Iron and Nickel

Types of Volcanoes and Rocks

Type of Volcano	Mode of Eruption	Types of rocks formed
Sheild Volcano	Does not Erupt, lava flows up and pours down slowly	Rock Basalt
Strato Volcano	Erupts with a violent explosion – hurling tons of hot igneous rock, ash and gas into the air	Rhyolite
Cinder Cone Volcano	Erupts by splattering big piles of ash and lava	Rhyolite and Pumice

Activity 1: The Rock Cycle Mind Map

Refer to the below pictorial map explaining the rock cycle including the various processes and create your own map that will help you remember them always!

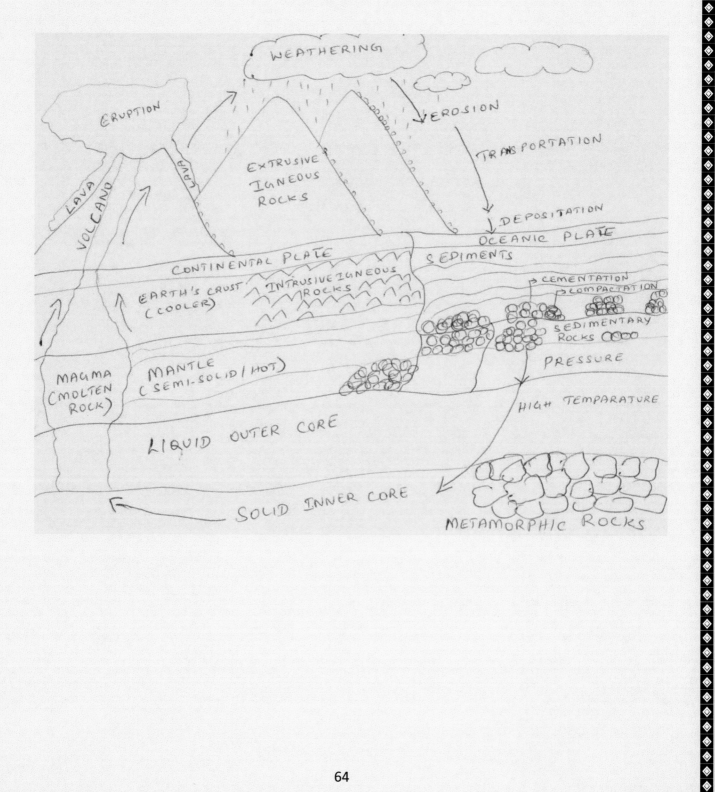

Activity 2: The Rock Cycle Quiz

1. Earth's core is extremely cold. True or False?

Answer:

2. What are the different rock categories?

Answer:

3. When a rock is formed as the result of lava cooling down, what is it called?

Answer:

4. Which type(s) of rock contain(s) fossils?

Answer:

5. What is molten rock called?

Answer:

6. Marble is a metamorphic rock. True or False?

Answer:

7. Rock cycle is a very quick process. True or False?

Answer:

8. Granite is a sedimentary rock – True or False?

Answer:

9. What are the different layers of Earth?

Answer:

Activity 3: The Rock Cycle Word Game

```
C  n  o  i  t  a  t  r  o  p  s  n  a  r  T
r  u  i  l  v  x  q  f  b  M  m  i  n  g  n
y  g  n  i  r  e  h  t  a  e  W  y  o  h  q
s  a  v  w  s  j  v  r  w  t  g  n  i  y  l
t  S  e  d  i  m  e  n  t  a  r  y  s  o  g
a  q  g  n  i  t  c  a  p  m  o  C  o  h  n
l  n  o  i  t  p  u  r  E  o  y  i  r  d  e
l  u  b  s  h  i  j  w  b  r  g  c  E  x  o
i  d  d  c  j  m  o  l  p  p  v  u  s  u  u
z  c  a  t  y  p  y  n  w  h  l  a  m  l  s
a  z  f  e  d  j  q  e  u  i  e  m  q  p  g
t  f  d  q  g  h  t  m  t  c  v  y  l  g  s
i  g  n  i  t  n  e  m  e  C  p  u  p  v  m
o  u  s  x  o  x  j  o  h  d  f  t  d  k  y
n  l  c  w  b  d  h  w  b  q  u  c  m  x  F
```

Find the below words on the above word square.

1. Igneous
2. Sedimentary
3. Metamorphic
4. Weathering
5. Eruption

6. Crystallization
7. Transportation
8. Compacting
9. Cementing
10. Erosion

Activity 4: Color and name the Rock Cycle Processes

1. Color and identify the layers of Earth, rock cycle processes and types of rocks

2. Enjoy coloring the shield volcano eruption.

6. Learn about the Landforms

The Landforms Song

The Earth is made up of Water and Land

To learn more about this, come join the landform band

There is water, water and water abound

And there are rocks, tress, gravel, clay and sand

This is the landform band

Let's sing together – hand in hand

And if you want a score that's grand

Sing along – this is your magic wand

Landforms are features of the Earth's surface

Landscapes and waterscapes are both in this trace

Plate movements, erosion and deposition cause the Earth to change face

Elevation, slope, soil and size determine the name the landform will embrace

Continent is a large land mass with water or land on the sides

Island is a land with water on all sides

Archipelago is the name for islands in clusters

A narrow land strip between water connecting landmasses is Isthmus

This is the landform band

Let's sing together – hand in hand

And if you want a score that's grand

Sing along – this is your magic wand

Land surrounded by water on three sides and land on one is a Peninsula

Tropical grassland with shrubs and scattered trees is a Savanna

Landform at the river mouth is called Delta

Vast, flat land with frozen subsoil is called Tundra

Rainforest is a warm, thick jungle that gets a lot of rain

Vast, flat grassland is called a Plain

Elevation of Earth that's much higher than the surrounding land is a Mountain

The landform rich in sediments drained by a river is called a Basin

This is the landform band

Let's sing together – hand in hand

And if you want a score that's grand

Sing along – this is your magic wand

An Ocean is a very large body of saline water

Cape is a pointed piece of land sticking into water

Large mass of slowly moving ice is a Glacier

Large stream of fresh water is called a River

Hills of sand made by wind is a Dune

A deep valley between cliffs is a Canyon

Desert is an arid land with rainfall close to none

Hill is the name for a less steep mountain

This is the landform band

Let's sing together – hand in hand

And if you want a score that's grand

Sing along – this is your magic wand

An isolated flat-topped hill with steep sides is a Mesa

And a Butte is a much smaller Mesa

Saline water mostly surrounded by land is a Bay

And a Gulf is a large bay

Valley is a low land between hills

Going very close to a huge waterfall may give you the chills

Volcano is a hill that frequently does lava spewing drills

Harbor is a protected body of water that shelters ships from perils

This is the landform band

Let's sing together – hand in hand

And if you want a score that's grand

Sing along – this is your magic wand

Beach is the land along the shoreline

To call Low-lying, water logged land as Marsh is fine

Cave is a large underground chamber in a hillside with no sunshine

Salt water separated from the sea by sandbank is called Lagoon

The pointed top of the mountain is a Peak

Cliff is a vertical rock that doesn't easily break

Large body of still fresh water is called a Lake

A pond is a mini lake and that's piece of cake!

This is the landform band

Let's sing together – hand in hand

And if you want a score that's grand

Sing along – this is your magic wand

Landforms: The Fact Sheet

What is Landform?

Landforms are natural features of the landscape, natural physical features of the earth's surface. Landforms are typically categorized by the physical attributes such as elevation, slope, orientation, rock exposure, and soil type etc. Though they are called landforms, the landform elements include landscapes as well as seascapes/water bodies.

Landform – Facts

- The study of landforms is called **Geomorphology**.
- Oceans and continents are the highest-order landforms
- A number of factors, ranging from Plate tectonics to erosion and deposition, can generate and affect landforms
- Many of the landform names are not restricted to refer to features of the planet Earth, and can be used to describe surface features of other planets and similar objects in the Universe.
- Landforms refer to any natural formation of rock, dirt and water.

Landscapes

Landform Name	Description	Name of Famous Landform/ Location	Other Information
Continents	A Continent is a large, continuous mass of land separated from other continents by water	Australia, North America, South America, Africa, Asia, Antarctica, Europe	Ural Mountains separate Europe and Asia – which is an exception to the definition of a Continent
Peninsula	A Peninsula is a piece of land almost surrounded by water or projecting out into a body of water. It is surrounded by water on 3 sides and land on one side	Indian Subcontinent, Asia	Florida is a well-known example of a large peninsula, with its land area divided between the larger Florida peninsula and the smaller Florida panhandle on the north and west.
Island	An Island is a piece of land that is surrounded by water on all sides	Greenland	A desert island is a small tropical island, where nobody lives or an undiscovered island.
Archipelago	An Archipelago is a cluster or chain of islands	Mergui Archipelago, Myanmar	Archipelagos are often volcanic, forming along island arcs generated by subduction zones or hotspots, but may also be the result of erosion, deposition and land elevation.

Landform Name	Description	Name of Famous Landform/ Location	Other Information
Cape	A *cape* is a pointed piece of land that sticks out into a sea, ocean, lake, or river	Cape Horn, South America	A cape is a geographical landform adjacent to water on three sides.
Isthmus	An Isthmus is a narrow strip of land with sea on either side, forming a link between two larger areas of land.	Kra Isthmus – Thailand and Myanmar	An Isthmus lies between two bodies of water and connects two larger land masses.
Plains	A Plain is a vast, flat grassland with very few trees which is lower than the land surrounding it	Salisbury Plain, England	Coastal plains generally rise from sea level until they meet higher landforms such as mountains or plateaus. Inland plains may be found at high altitudes. Prairies and Steppes are types of plains
Savanna	A savanna is a grassland scattered with shrubs and isolated trees	Serengeti Plains, Tanzania	Savannas are also known as tropical grasslands. They have very wet summers and very dry winters

Landform Name	Description	Name of Famous Landform/ Location	Other Information
Tundra	Tundra is a vast, flat, treeless Arctic region in which the subsoil is permanently frozen.	Arctic Tundra, Northern Hemisphere Antarctic Tundra, Southern Hemisphere Alpine Tundra - American Cordillera, North and South America	Tundra is an extremely cold and windy area
Delta	A delta is a landform that is formed at the mouth of a river, where that river flows into an ocean, sea, estuary, lake, or reservoir.	Nile River Delta, Egypt	Deltas are formed from the deposition of the sediment carried by the river as the flow leaves the mouth of the river.
Plateau	A Plateau is an area of highland that is usually very flat	Colorado Plateau, USA	Plateaus can be formed by a number of processes, including upwelling of volcanic magma, extrusion of lava, and erosion by water and glaciers.

Landform Name	Description	Name of Famous Landform/ Location	Other Information
Valley	A Valley is a low area of land between hills or mountains, typically with a river or stream flowing through it.	Yosemite Valley, USA	A valley in its broadest geographic sense is also known as a *Dale.* A valley through which a river runs may also be referred to as a **Vale**. A small, secluded, and often wooded valley is known as a **dell**. A wide, flat valley through which a river runs is known as a **Strath**. A mountain **cove** is a small valley, closed at one or both ends. A small valley surrounded by mountains or ridges is sometimes known as a **hollow**. A deep, narrow valley is known as a **coon.**
Basin	A Basin is a region drained by a river and its tributaries – a low-lying area on the Earth's surface in which thick layers of sediment have accumulated.	Wyoming Basin, USA	Geologic faults can often occur around the edge of, and within, the basin, as a result of the ongoing slippage and subsidence.

Landform Name	Description	Name of Famous Landform/ Location	Other Information
Rainforest	A *rainforest* is a warm, thick jungle that gets a lot of rain. A large number of plants and animals live there	Amazon Rainforest, Brazil	Rainforests can be found in Asia, Australia, Africa, South America, Central America, Mexico and on many of the Pacific, Caribbean, and Indian Ocean islands.
Desert	A Desert is an arid landscape that receives meager rainfall that supports very little or no vegetation	Sahara - Morocco, Western Sahara, Algeria, Tunisia, Libya, Egypt, Mauritania, Mali, Niger, Chad, Ethiopia, Eritrea, Somalia Antarctic Desert – Antarctica	About one-third of Earth's surface is covered by deserts Hot deserts are covered with Sand and cold deserts are covered with Snow and Ice
Oasis	An Oasis is a small area in a desert that has a supply of water and is able to support vegetation.	Ubari Lake Oasis/ Libya	An oasis forms when groundwater lies close enough to the surface to form a spring or to be reached by wells.
Dunes	A *Dune* is a hill of sand built by wind	Moreeb Hill - UAE (near Liwa Oasis, Abu Dhabi)	Sand dunes form in beaches also There are five basic types of dunes: *Crescentic*, *Linear*, *Star*, *Dome*, and *Parabolic*.

Mountainous Landforms

Landform Name	Description	Name of Famous Landform/ Location	Other Information
Mountain	A Mountain is large natural elevation of the earth's surface rising abruptly from the surrounding level	Alps Mountain Range, Europe	There are five major types of Mountains - Fold, Fault-block, Volcanic, Dome, Plateau
Hill	A **hill** is a landform that extends above the surrounding terrain.	Seven Hills of Rome, Italy	The distinction between a hill and a mountain is unclear and largely subjective, but a hill is generally somewhat lower and less steep than a mountain
Peak	A Peak is the pointed top of a mountain.	Mount Everest, Asia	The term "summit" is generally used for a mountain peak
Cliff	A C**liff** is a significant vertical, or near vertical, rock exposure.	Trango Towers, Pakistan	Cliffs are formed due to the processes of erosion and weathering. Cliffs are common on coasts, in mountainous areas, escarpments and along rivers.
Butte	A Butte is an isolated hill with steep sides and a flat top	Merrick's Butte in Monument Valley, Utah	A Butte is smaller than mesas, plateaus.

Landform Name	Description	Name of Famous Landform/ Location	Other Information
Canyon	A **Canyon** or **G**orge is a deep valley between cliffs often carved from the landscape by a river.	Grand Canyon, Arizona	Most canyons were formed by a process of long-time erosion from a plateau level. Canyons are much more common in arid areas than in wet areas because physical weathering has a greater effect in arid zones.
Mesa	A Mesa is an isolated flat-topped hill with steep sides	Tucumcari Mountain - New Mexico, USA	Mesas are formed by weathering and erosion of horizontally layered rocks that have been uplifted by tectonic activity.
Volcano	A *Volcano* is a conical hill or mountain formed by material from the mantle being forced through an opening or vent in the Earth's crust.	Mount Etna - Sicily, Italy	Volcanoes are generally found where tectonic plates are diverging or converging. A mid-oceanic ridge, for example the Mid-Atlantic Ridge, has examples of volcanoes caused by divergent tectonic plates pulling apart; the Pacific Ring of Fire has examples of volcanoes caused by convergent tectonic plates coming together.

Landform Name	Description	Name of Famous Landform/ Location	Other Information
Cave	A Cave is a large underground chamber, typically of natural origin, in a hillside or cliff.	Lechuguilla Cave, New Mexico	Speleology is the science of exploration and study of all aspects of caves and the environment which surrounds the caves.

Glacial Landforms

Landform Name	Description	Name of Famous Landform/ Location	Other Information
Glacier	A Glacier is a large mass of snow/ice moving slowly over the landmass	Malaspina Glacier on Yakutat Bay, Alaska	Regions with continuous snowfall and constant freezing temperatures foster the development of Glaciers/frozen rivers
Fjord	A Fjord is a long, narrow inlet with steep sides or cliffs on three sides, created in a valley carved by glacial activity	Scoresby Sund, Greenland	The opening toward the sea is called the mouth of the Fjord, and is often shallow. The Fjord's inner part is called the sea bottom. If the geological formation is wider than it is long, it is not a Fjord. Then it is a bay or cove

Landform Name	Description	Name of Famous Landform/ Location	Other Information
Cirques	A Cirque is a bowl shaped hollow at the head of a valley. Within a cirque lies a snowfield, the place where snow accumulates to form a cirque glacier.	Corrie Glacier, Alaska	Glaciers make cirques by grinding existing valleys into a rounded shape with steep sides.

Waterscapes

Landform Name	Description	Name of Famous Landform/ Location	Other Information
Ocean	An Ocean is a very large body of saline water covering a huge part of the Earth	Pacific Ocean Atlantic Ocean Indian Ocean Southern Ocean Arctic Ocean	Though generally described as several 'separate' oceans, these all water bodies comprise one global, interconnected body of salt water sometimes referred to as the World Ocean or global ocean.

Landform Name	Description	Name of Famous Landform/ Location	Other Information
Sea	A sea is a large body of saline water that is partially enclosed by land	Coral Sea, near Australia	Seas are smaller than oceans and are usually located where the land and ocean meet. Typically, seas are partially enclosed by land.
Bay	A bay is an area of saline water mostly surrounded by land.	Bay of Bengal, South Asia	Bays generally have calmer waters than the surrounding sea, due to the surrounding land blocking some waves and often reducing winds.
Gulf	A Gulf is a large bay that is an arm of an ocean or sea.	Gulf of Alaska, Pacific Ocean	Meteorologically, the Gulf is a great generator of storms.
Cove	A cove is a small circular or oval coastal inlet with a narrow entrance.	McWay Cove – California, USA	Some Coves may be referred to as Bays.
Channel	A channel is the physical confine of a river, slough or ocean strait consisting of a bed and banks.	The English Channel – England and France	A channel is also the natural or human-made deeper course through a reef, sand bar, bay, or any shallow body of water.

Landform Name	Description	Name of Famous Landform/ Location	Other Information
Trench	Oceanic trenches are long but narrow topographic depressions of the sea floor.	Mariana Trench, Pacific ocean	Oceanic trenches typically extend 3 to 4 km (1.9 to 2.5 mi) below the level of the surrounding oceanic floor.
Lagoon	A Lagoon is a stretch of salt water separated from the sea by a low sandbank or coral reef.	Glenrock Lagoon, Australia	Lagoons that are fed by freshwater streams are also called Estuaries
Strait	A Strait is a narrow passage of navigable water connecting two seas or two large areas of water.	The Strait of Gibraltar – Atlantic Ocean and Mediterranean Sea	Straits lie between two land masses and connect two larger bodies of water
Harbor	A *Harbor* is a protected body of water that can be used as a shelter for ships.	San Francisco Bay – CA, USA	A large harbor is often combined with a port - a facility which allows ships to load and unload cargo.
River	A River is a large natural stream of fresh water flowing in a channel to the sea, a lake, or another stream.	Amazon River, Brazil	Potamology is the scientific study of rivers A small narrow, river is called a Stream

Landform Name	Description	Name of Famous Landform/ Location	Other Information
Tributary	A Tributary is a smaller river or stream flowing into a larger river or lake.	Tigre, Peruvian Tributary of the Amazon river	A tributary does not flow directly into a sea. A confluence, where two or more bodies of water meet together, usually refers to the joining of tributaries.
Lake	A *Lake* is a body of mostly still fresh or salt water of considerable size, localized in a basin, that is surrounded by land	Great Salt Lake – Utah, USA	Lakes are inland and not part of the ocean and therefore are distinct from lagoons, and are larger and deeper than ponds.
Pond	A Pond is a fairly small body of still water surrounded by land	Walden Pond – Massachusetts, USA	Ponds can be natural or artificially created
Waterfall	A Waterfall is a cascade of water falling from a height - formed when a river or stream flows over a steep incline.	Niagara Falls, Canada and USA	Streams become wider and shallower just above waterfalls due to flowing over the rock shelf, and there is usually a deep area just below the waterfall because of the kinetic energy of the water hitting the bottom.

Land / Waterscapes

Landform Name	Description	Name of Famous Landform/ Location	Other Information
Marsh/ Swamp	A Marsh is an area of low-lying land that is flooded in wet seasons or at high tide, and typically remains waterlogged at all times.	Marshlands – Charleston, United States	Two major types are – Salt water Marshes and Fresh Water Marshes
Beach	A B*each* is a landform along the shoreline of an ocean, sea, lake or river.	Tulum Beach, Mexico	Beaches typically occur in areas along the coast where wave or current action deposits and reworks sediments.
Atoll	An Atoll is a ring-shaped reef, island, or chain of islands formed of coral.	Huvadhu Atoll, Maldives	Atolls are the product of the growth of tropical marine organisms, and so these islands are only found in warm tropical waters.
Reef	A Reef is a ridge of jagged rock, coral, or sand just above or below the surface of the sea.	The Great Barrier Reef – Queensland, Australia	Coral reefs are underwater structures made from calcium carbonate secreted by corals.

Activity 1: The Landforms Mind Map

Refer to the below pictorial map capturing some of the Landforms and create your own map that will help you remember them always!

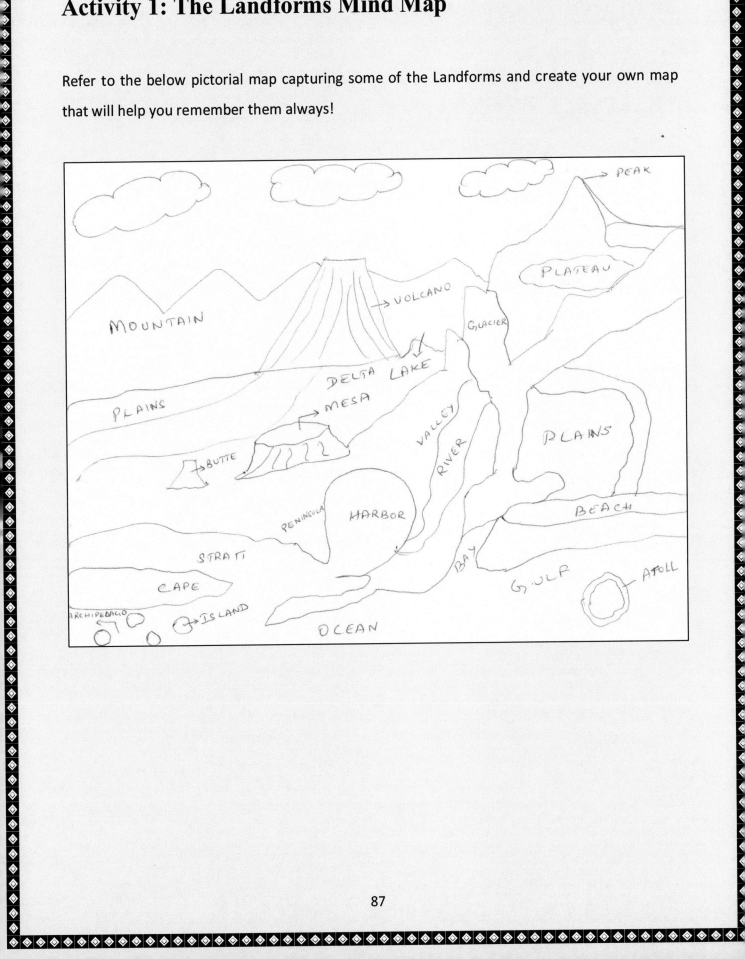

Activity 2: The Landform Quiz

1. Name a famous Glacier.

Answer:

2. Name the island Continent

Answer:

3. What is an Atoll?

Answer:

4. An area of highland that is mostly flat is called a …..

Answer:

5. A piece of land that is almost completely surrounded by water is called a ….

Answer:

6. Lowland between Mountains or Hills is a called a ……

Answer:

7. What is Tundra?

Answer:

8. What is a Lagoon?

Answer:

9. What is a Fjord?

Answer:

Activity 3: The Landforms Word Game

G	n	i	a	t	n	u	o	M	C	V	V	J	N	G
e	I	D	C	H	X	X	N	O	L	W	U	A	D	l
i	s	e	a	S	R	J	K	C	C	E	K	t	X	a
r	l	s	n	L	t	n	e	n	i	t	n	o	C	c
i	a	e	y	V	a	l	l	e	y	C	S	l	L	i
a	n	r	o	W	S	P	K	I	F	O	D	l	Y	e
r	d	t	n	I	B	V	H	P	S	Z	S	N	K	r
P	Z	X	V	B	E	E	T	F	Q	O	E	B	Y	W
W	O	B	J	Y	R	E	I	F	W	M	K	K	L	B
A	r	c	h	i	p	e	l	a	g	o	Q	X	B	F
B	O	E	O	V	G	D	F	I	F	G	X	Y	X	T
u	a	Q	X	Z	P	A	T	V	o	l	c	a	n	o
t	s	W	X	Q	H	S	a	v	a	n	n	a	h	S
t	i	V	Z	S	t	r	a	i	t	E	S	F	M	R
e	s	N	D	I	O	V	N	H	O	D	S	T	E	C

1. Volcano
2. Archipelago
3. Strait
4. Mountain
5. Continent
6. Island
7. Butte
8. Prairie
9. Savannah
10. Glacier

11. Desert
12. Oasis
13. Atoll
14. Canyon
15. Valley

Activity 4: Color and name the Landforms

Color and identify the Landforms.